Oceans and Abstracts

Michael Marschner

Copyright © 2020 Michael Marschner
All rights reserved.
ISBN: 9798621931551

DEDICATION

This work is dedicated to my wife, Maggie, without whom it would have been impossible.

Authors note: The images and poems in this book are my own. I take the photos so that I can use them to look at the world. I edit them so that I can attempt to understand how our seemingly solid and constant reality is in fact a shared illusion (after science has had its say.). I then write the poems to try and give it all a human meaning.

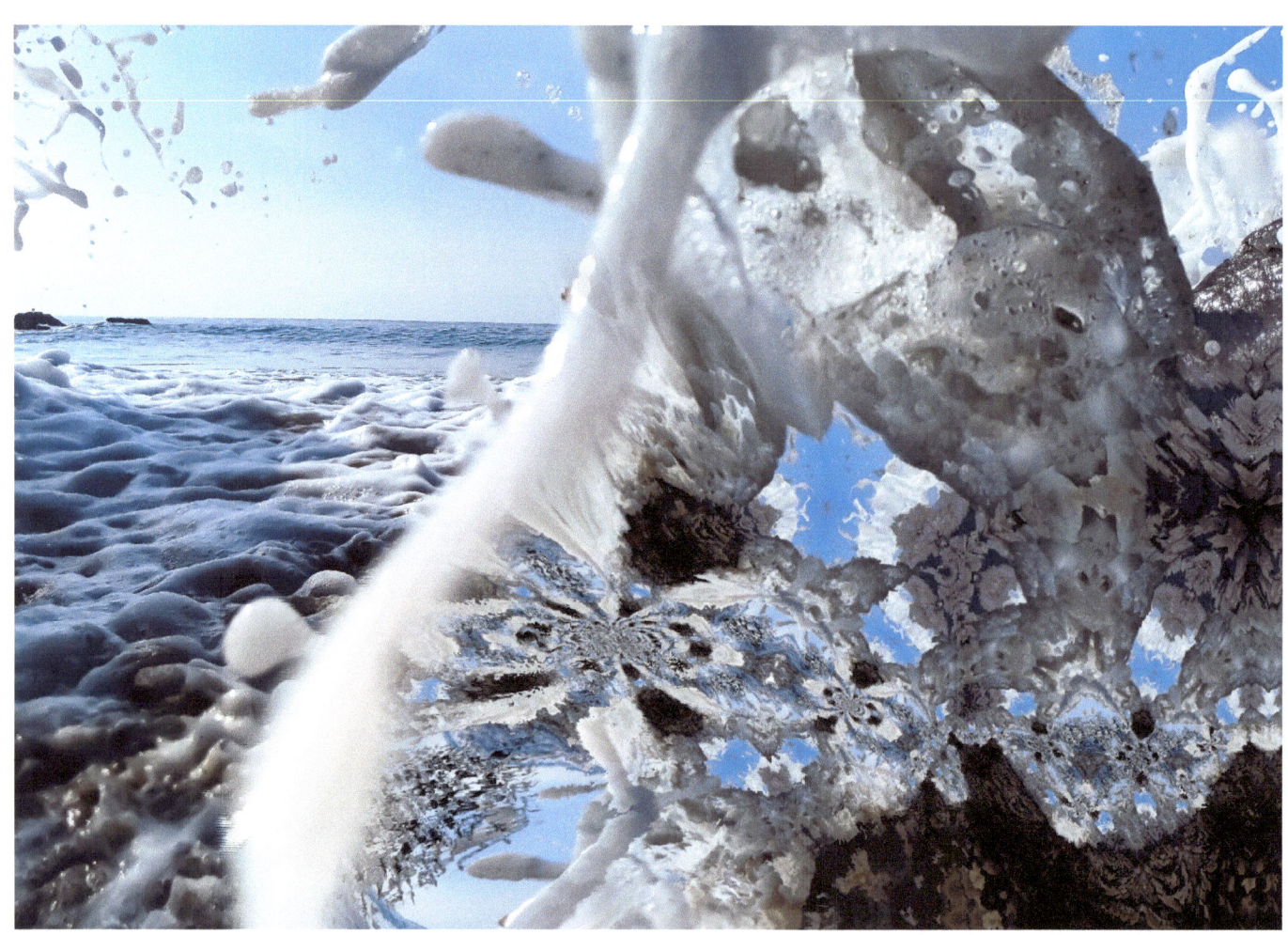

ABSTRACT WITH SURF, PCH CA

Every valuable human being must be a radical and a rebel, for what he must aim at is to make things better than they are.

-Niels Bohr

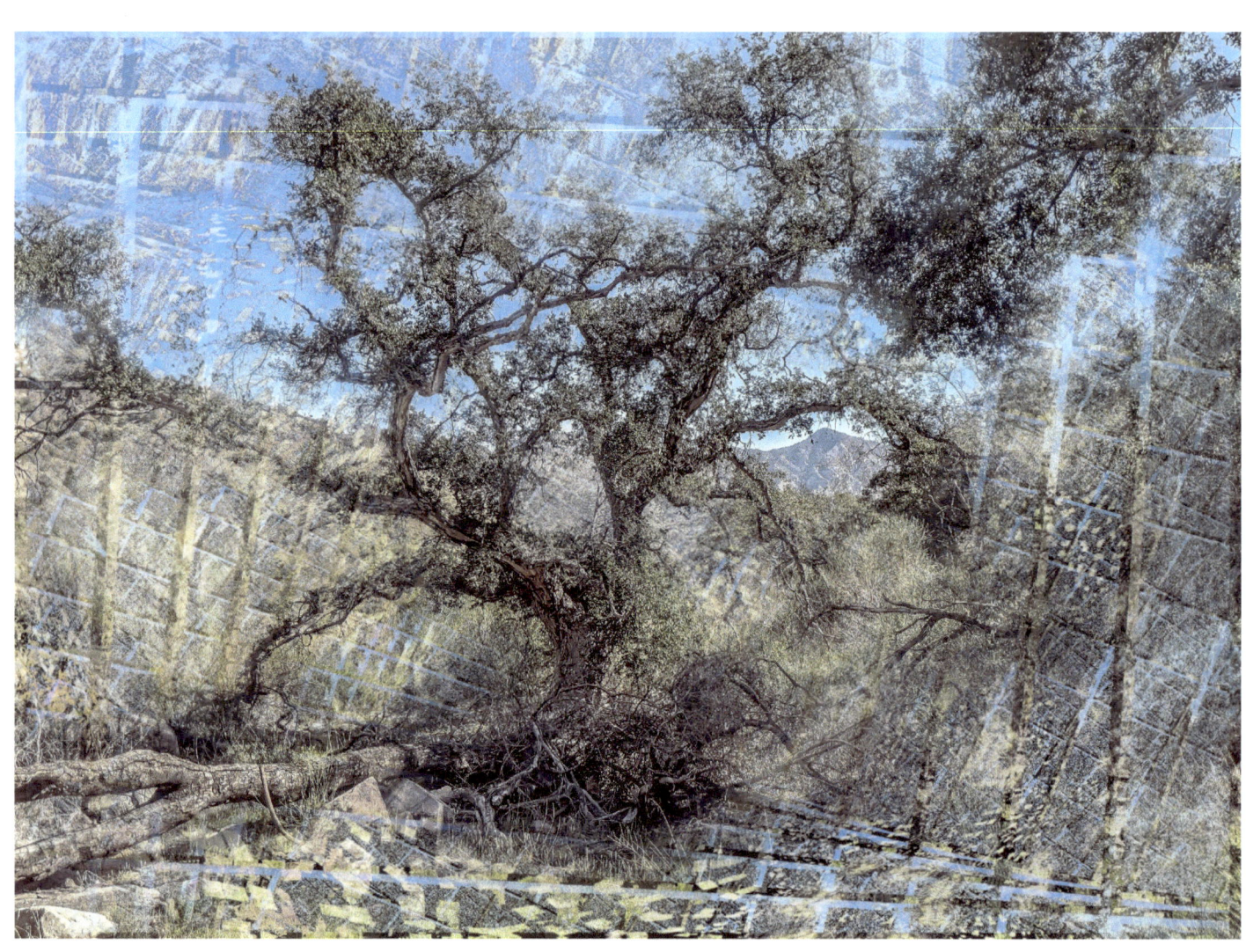

TREE NEAR SESPE CREEK, CA

To a Lonely Tree

Twisted branches
Bent by wind-
Gnarled trunk
Scarred by dry, drought, and fire-

Had but your seed fallen on different ground,
Well watered ground
Safe and sheltered ground
Then might your shape be as perfect as the ground.

But yours the shape of one who withstood
The efforts of the world to destroy.
Neither straight nor perfect - perhaps -
But certainly the more beautiful for that.

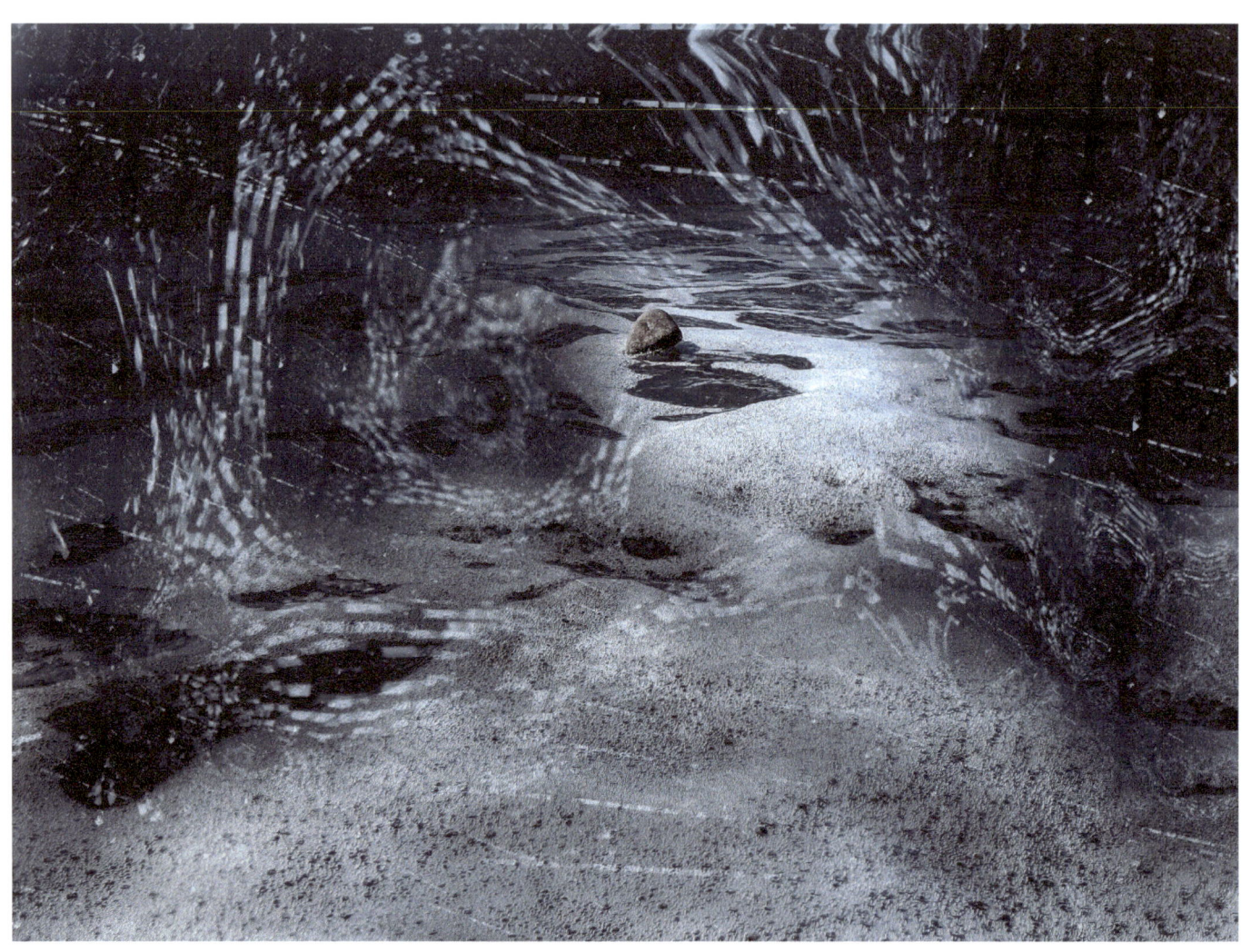

ABSTRACT WITH ROCK LANDING ON OCEAN WATER

It once was said:
Eventually all things merge together
And a river runs through it.

I have wondered oft,
Upon sleepless nights
Both care and sorrow driven
How such a thing could ever be
In a world by hatred driven.

Sleepless nights are cured by love,
So too are sorrows wounds.
Perhaps it can so too unite what our minds
Have torn asunder -
'ere Times river cease.

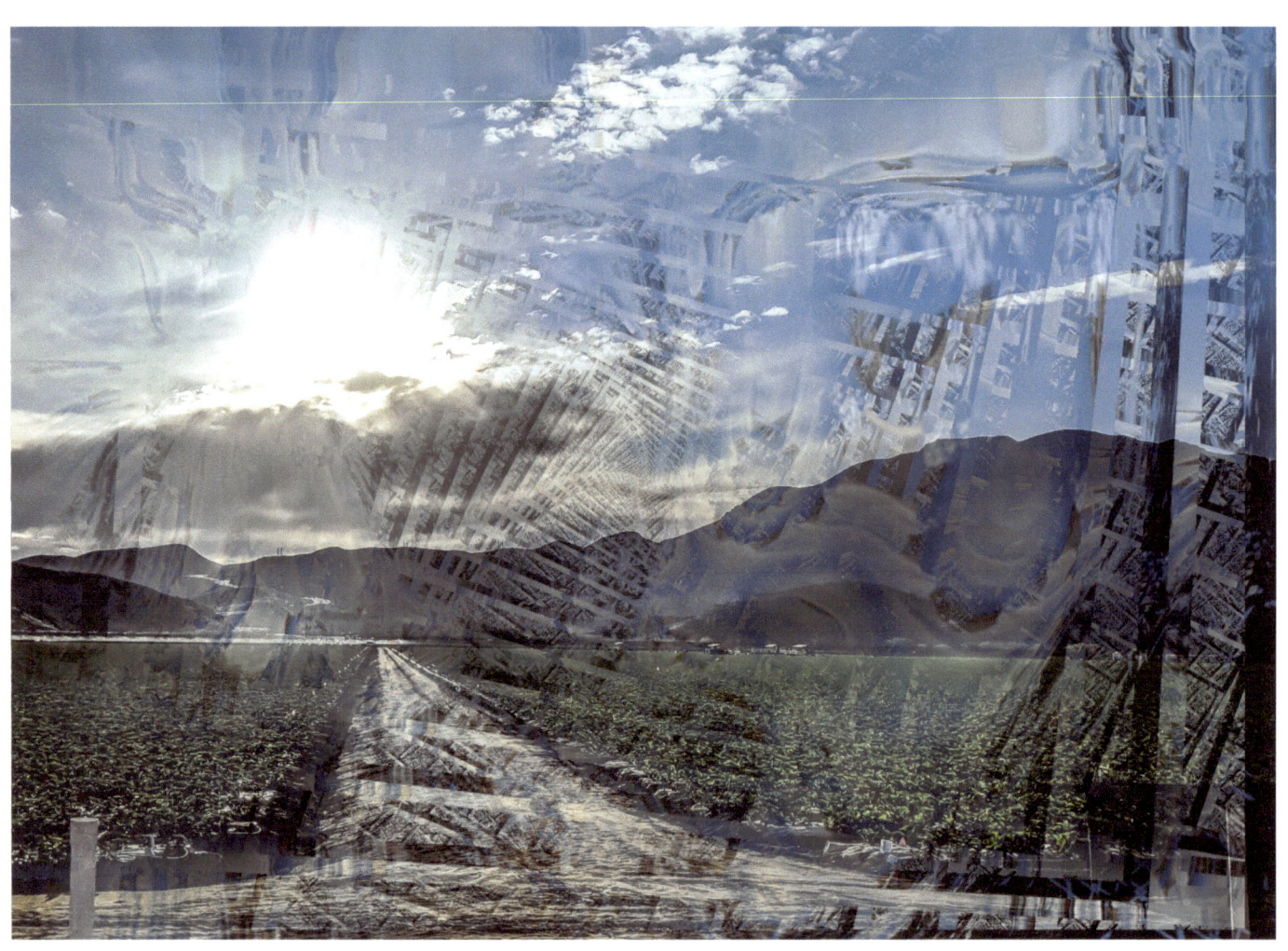

FARMERS FIELD, CAMARILLO CA

Since distant days,
Near lost in mists of time-

Before Egypt held sway o'er
Water and rock,
Or Rome held sway o'er
Body and soul

Have farmers fields been stained
Stained red with blood
By humans poured, from humans sourced.

Some was spilled for fear
The gods would grieve its lack.

Most was spilled for fear
That we have less than they.

Neither the land nor the gods want our blood,
And yet our blood still flows.
We seem to want the blood of others,
- till all have the same amount?

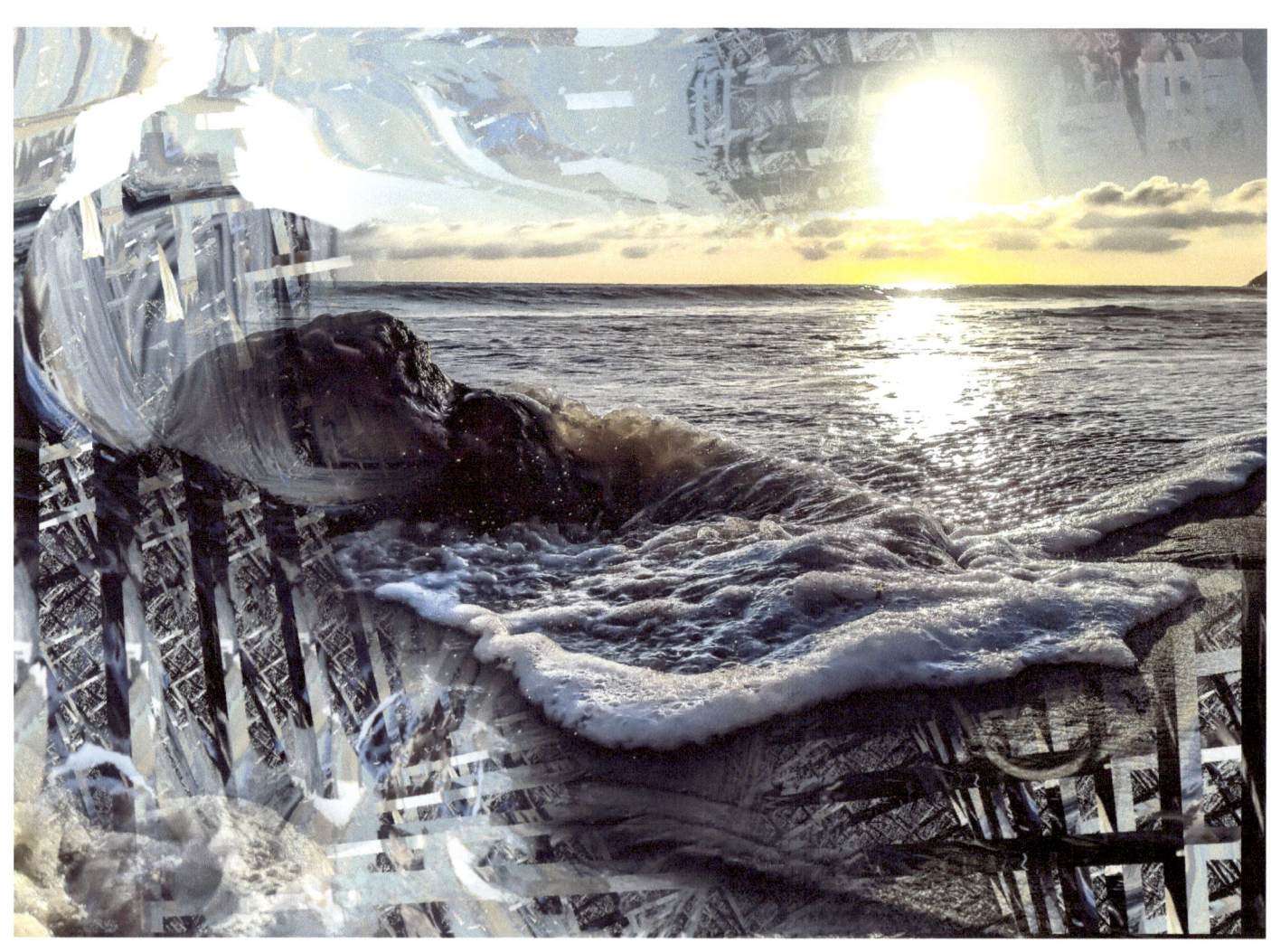

PACIFIC OCEAN SUNSET, CA

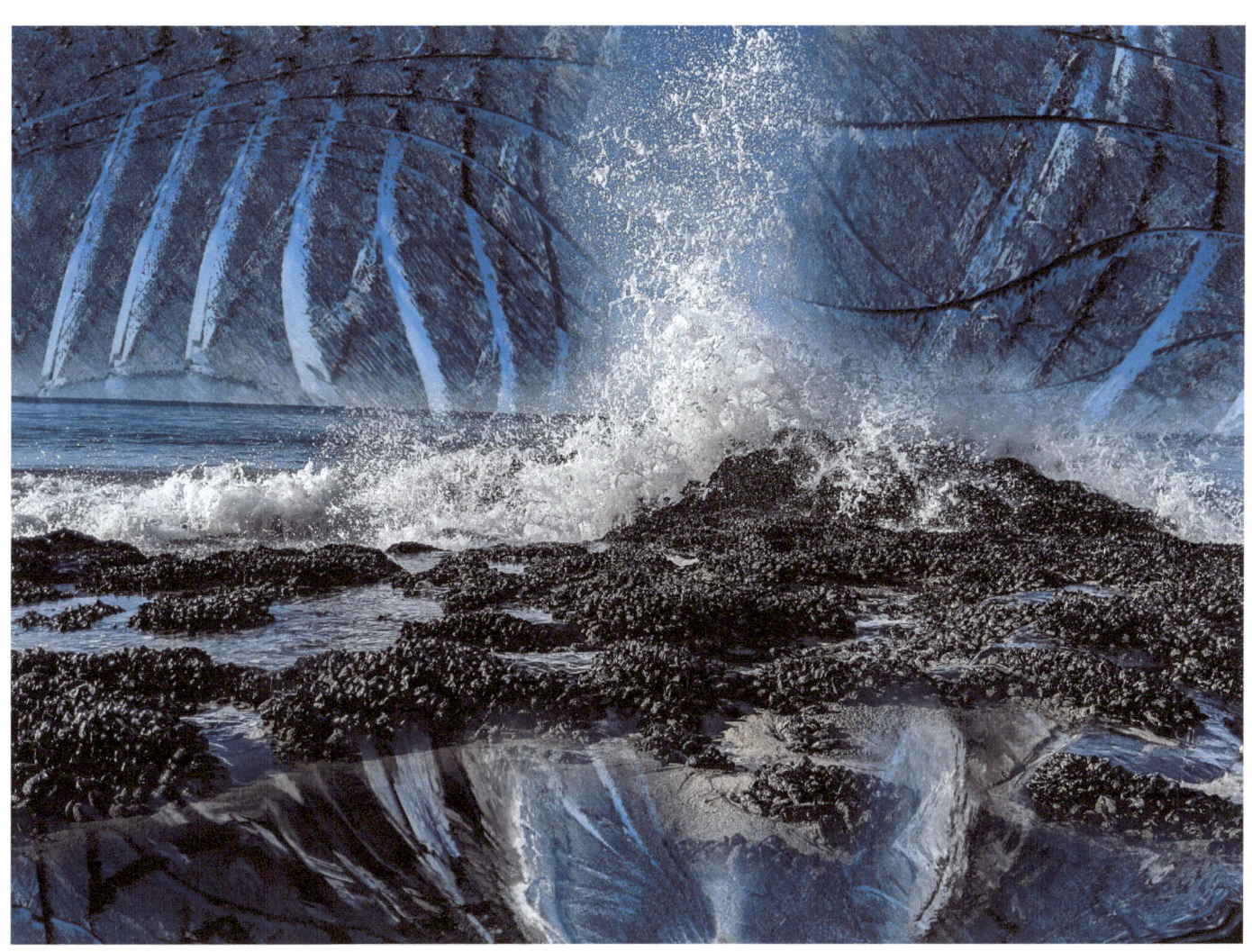

ABSTRACT WITH CRASHING WAVE I

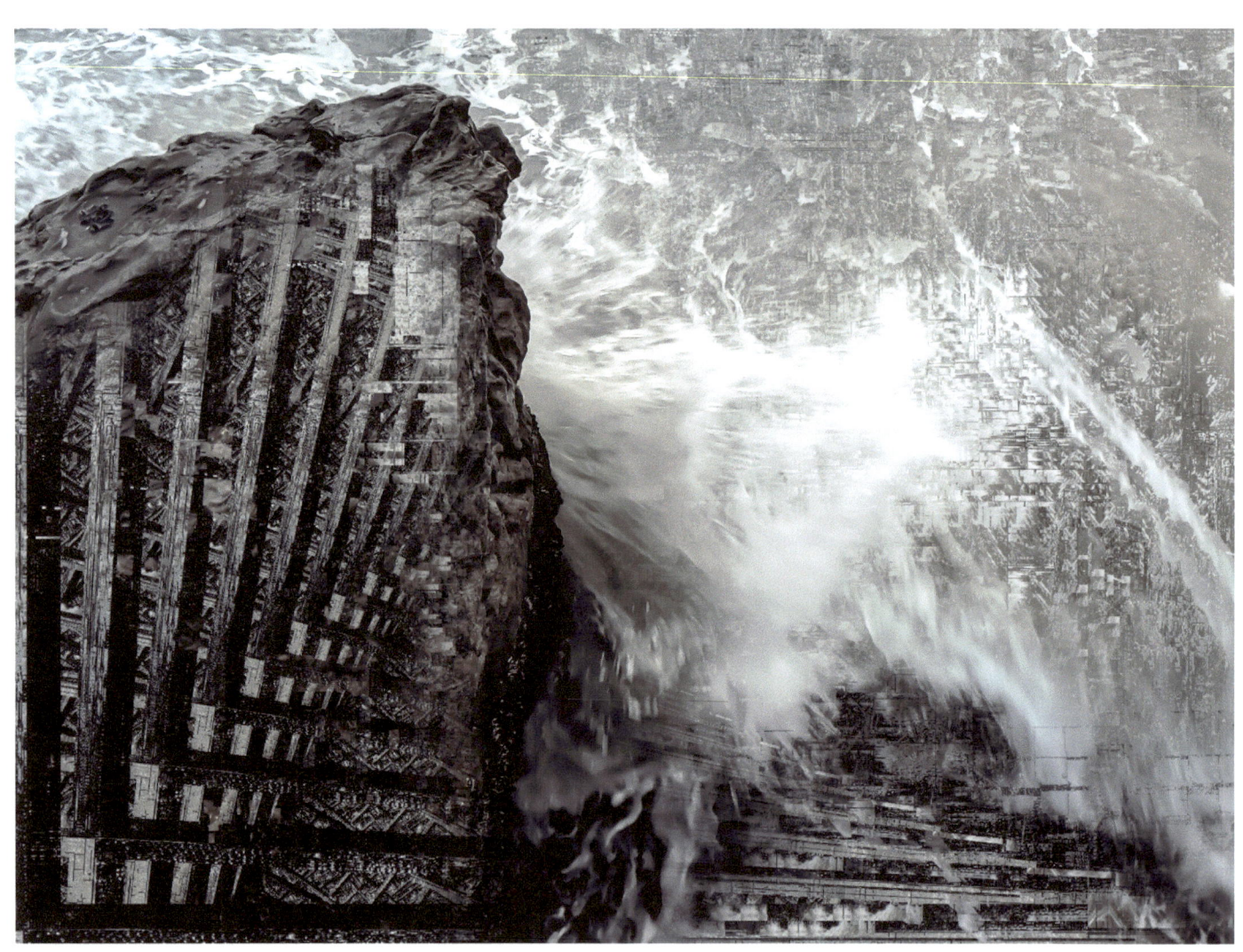

ABSTRACT WITH CRASHING WAVE II

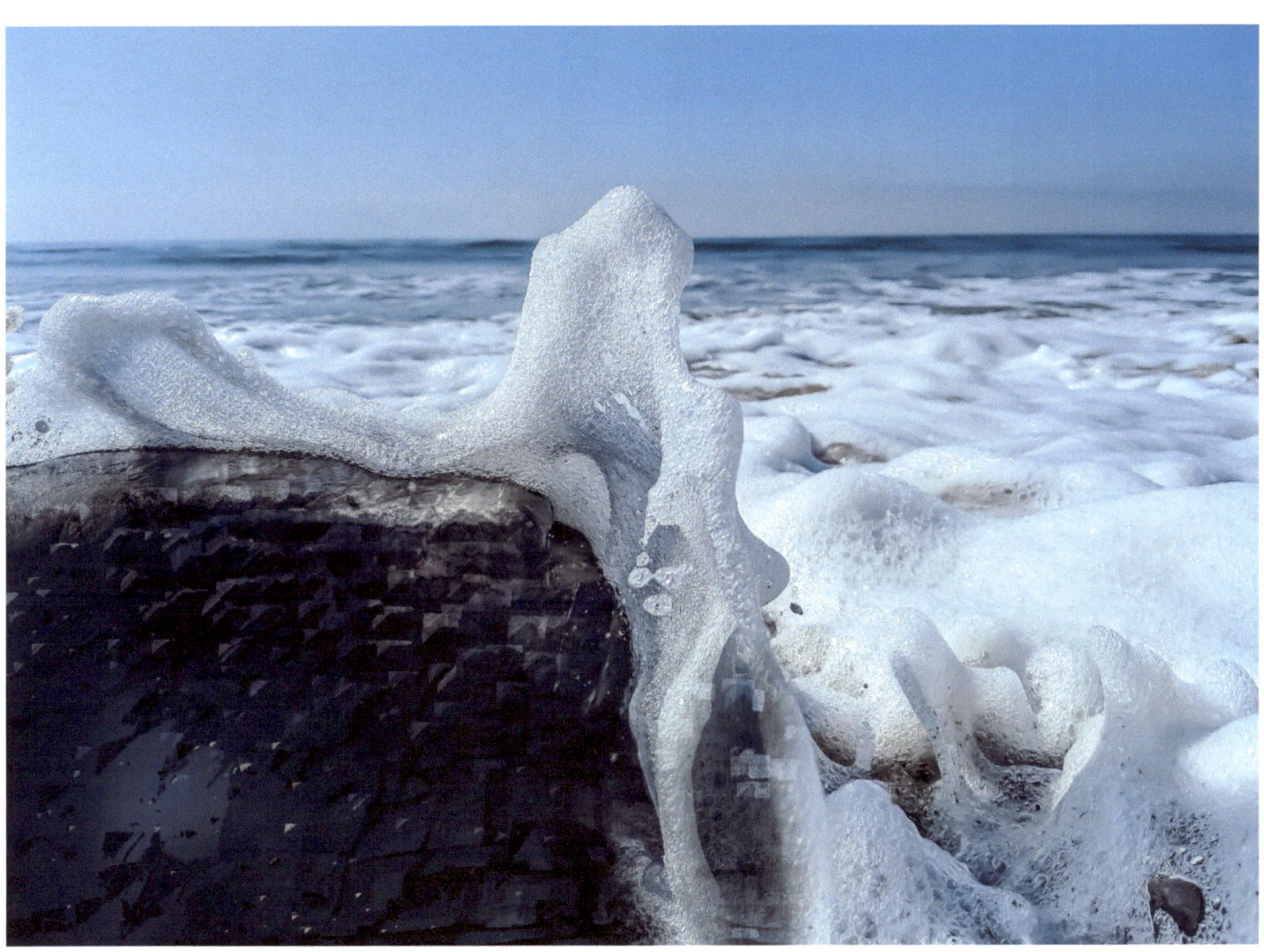

THE THING AND ITSELF

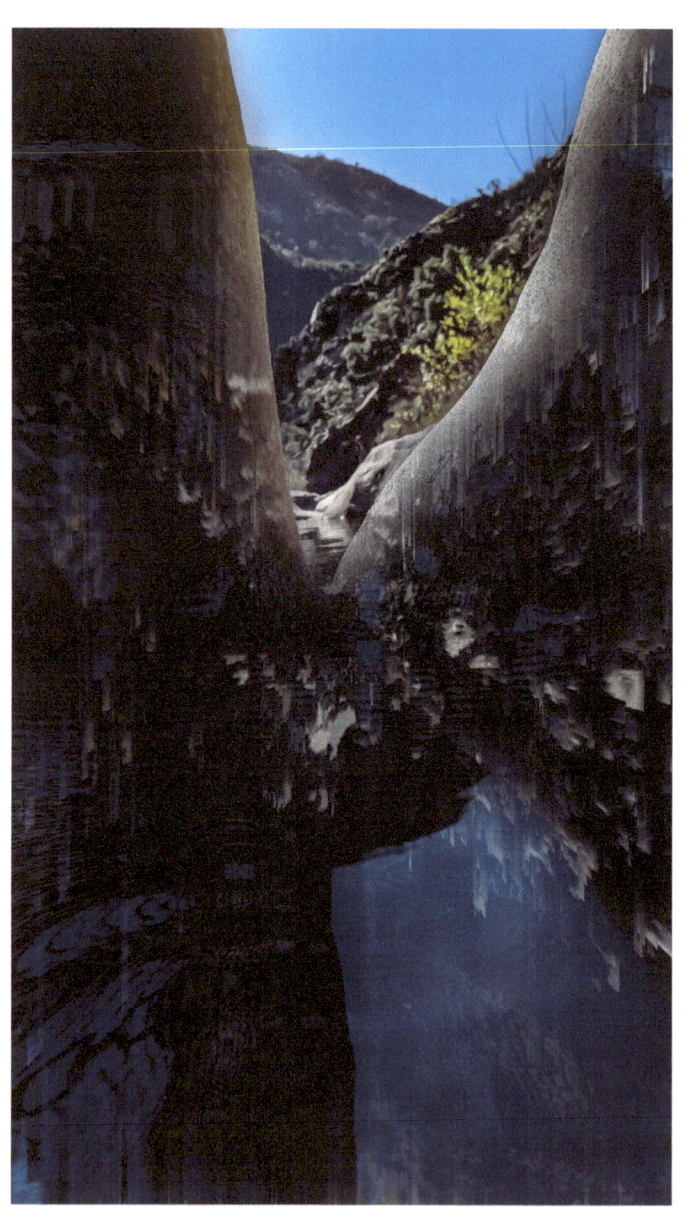 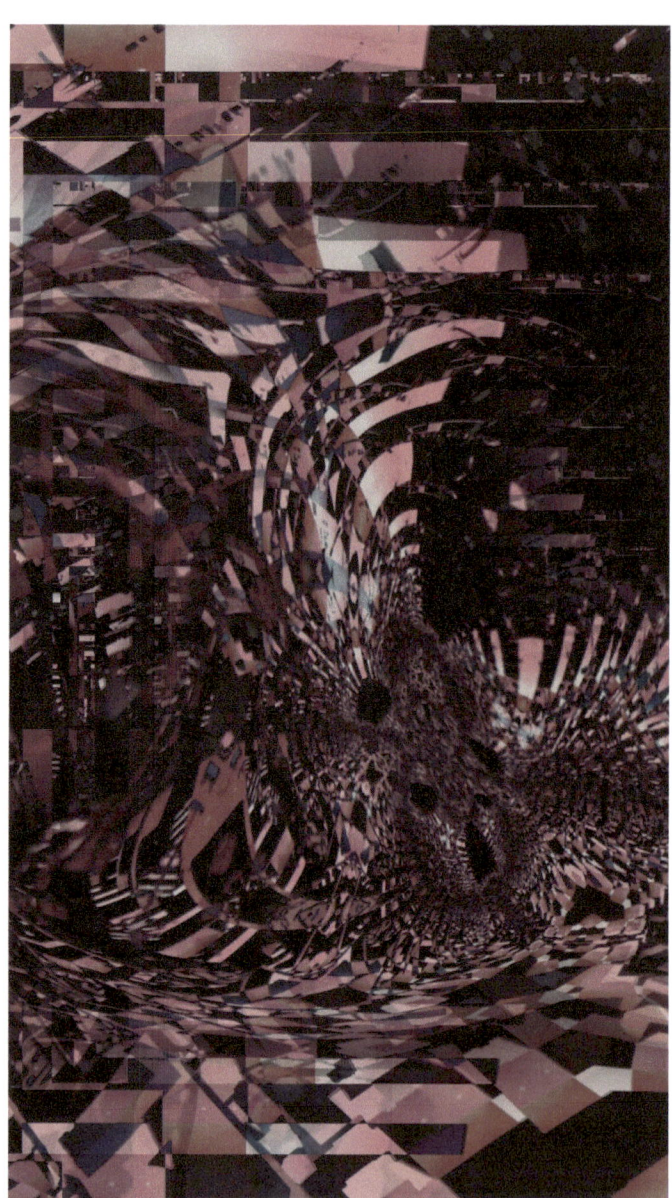

DECONSTRUCTING THE EXPLICATE ORDER　　　**ABSTRACT IN RED**

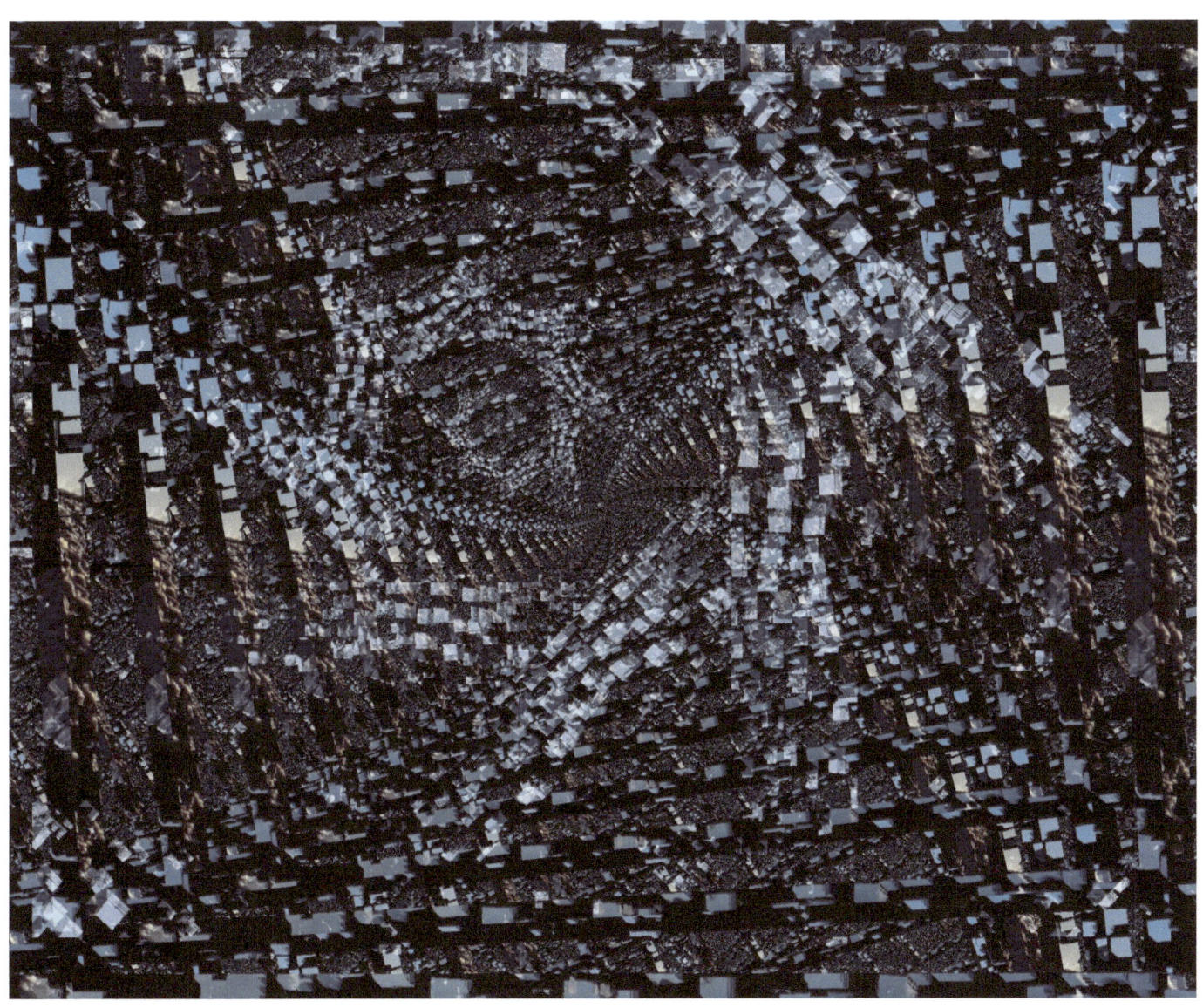

GHOST IN THE MACHINE

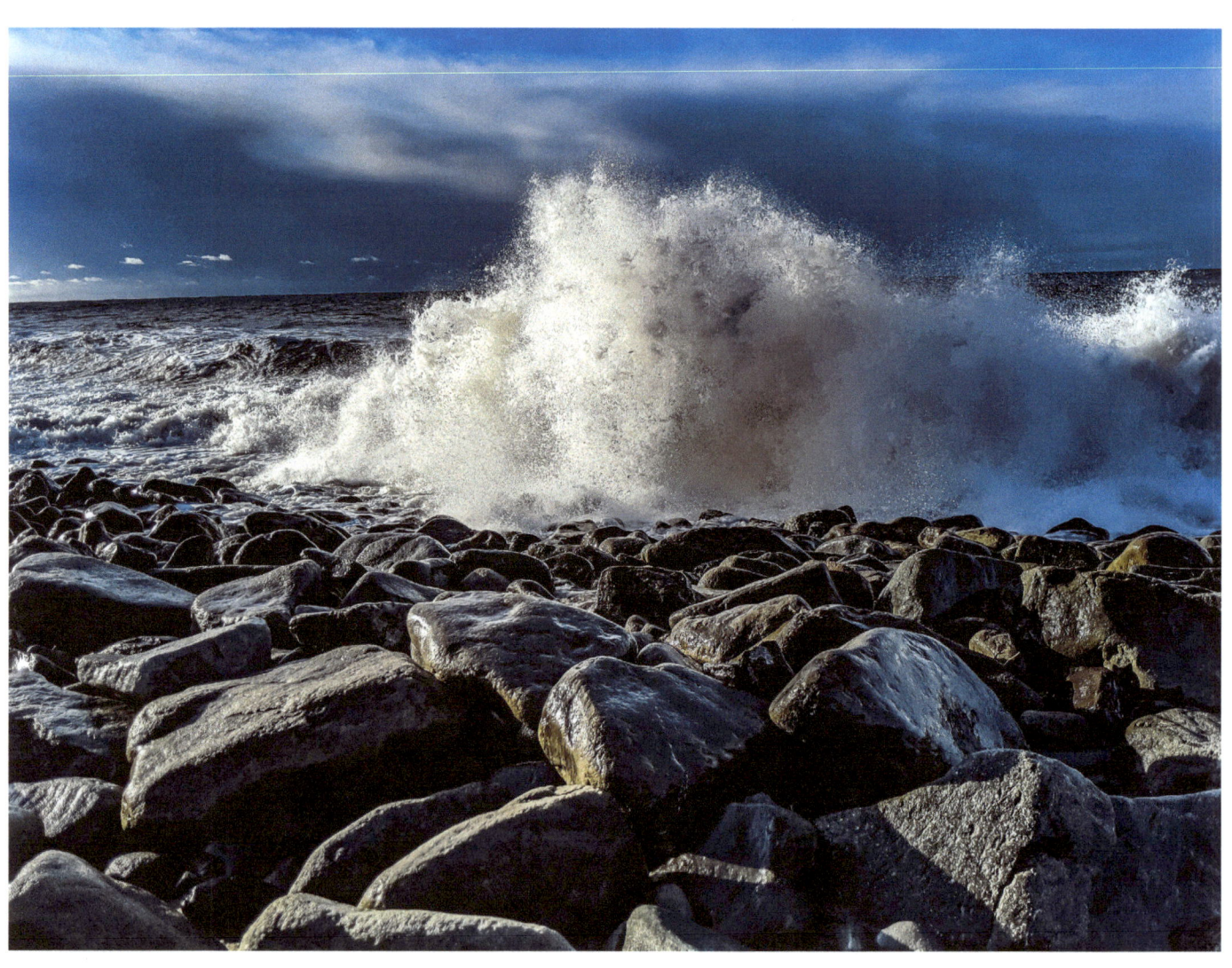

CRASHING WAVE, SYCAMORE COVE, CA

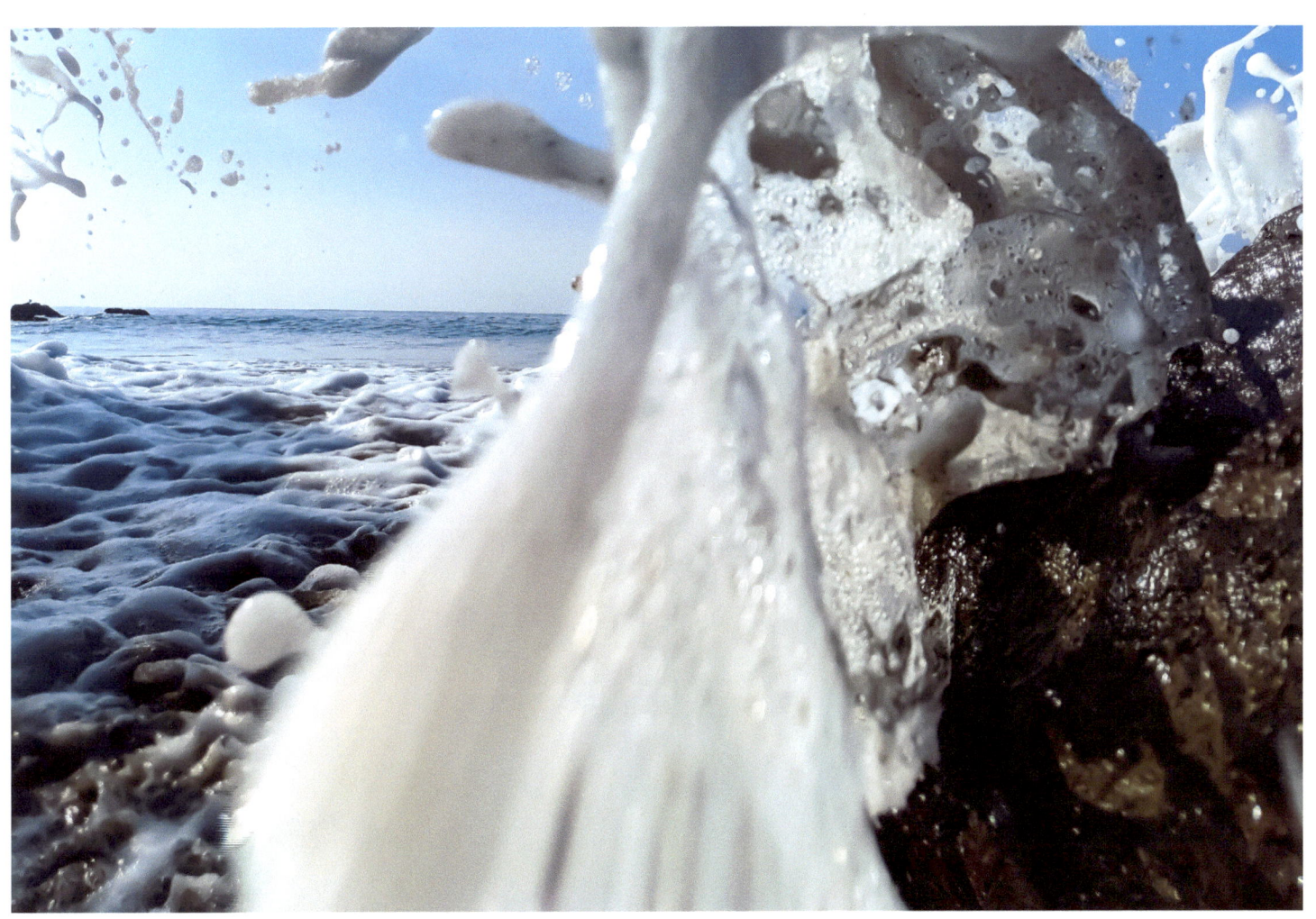

INCOMING SURF I, LEO CARILLO STATE PARK, CA

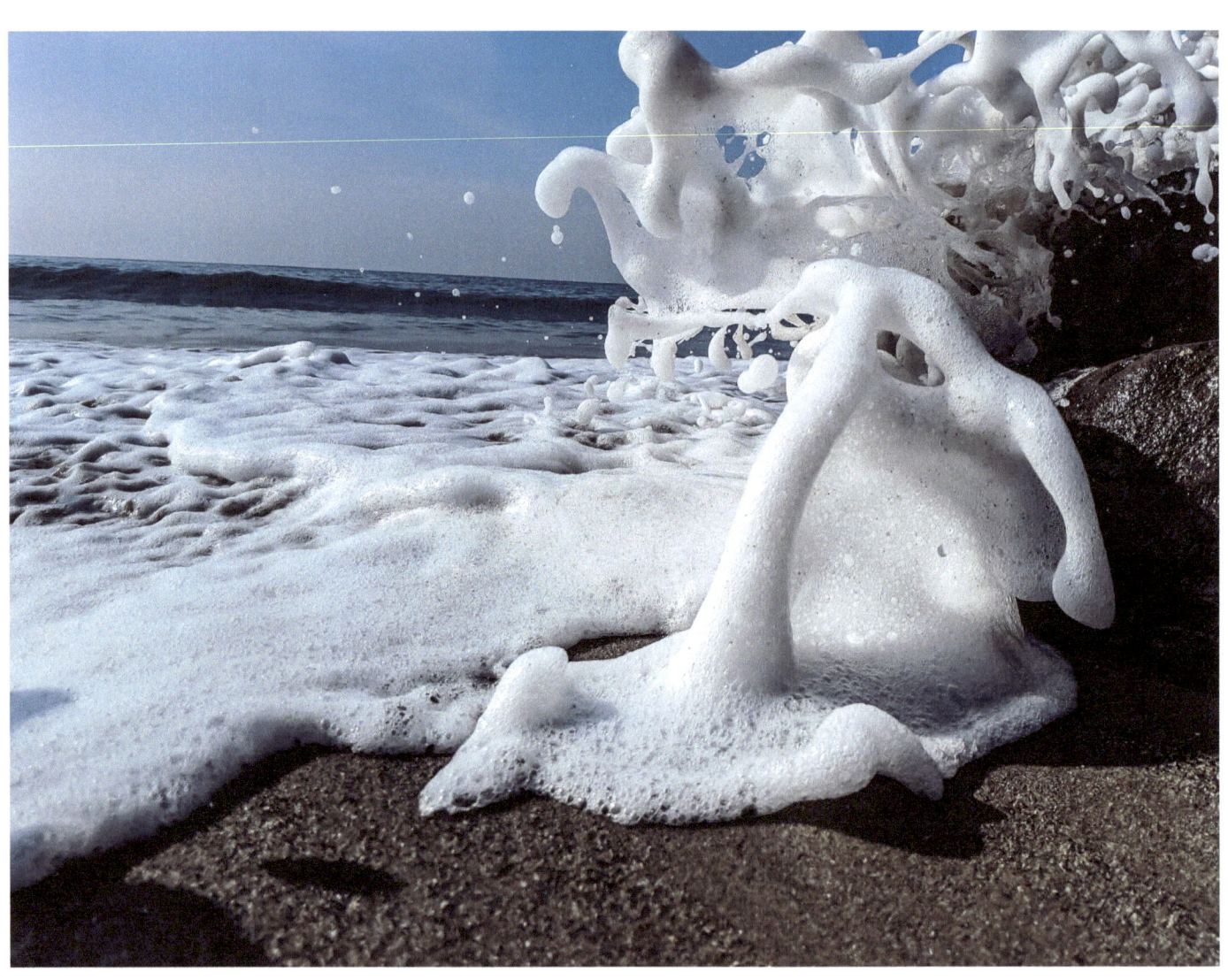

INCOMING SURF II, LEO CARILLO STATE PARK, CA

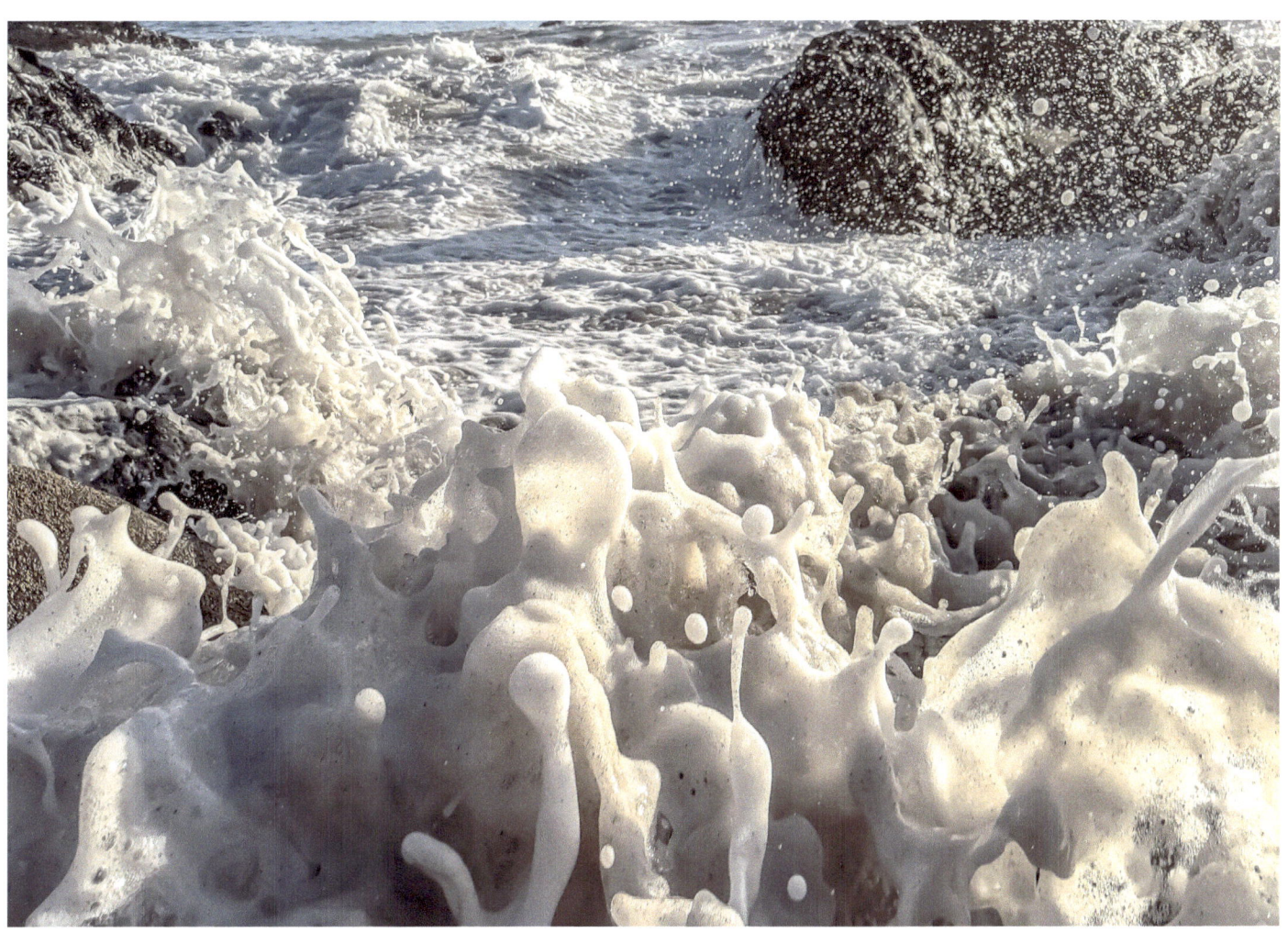

INCOMING SURF III, PCH CA

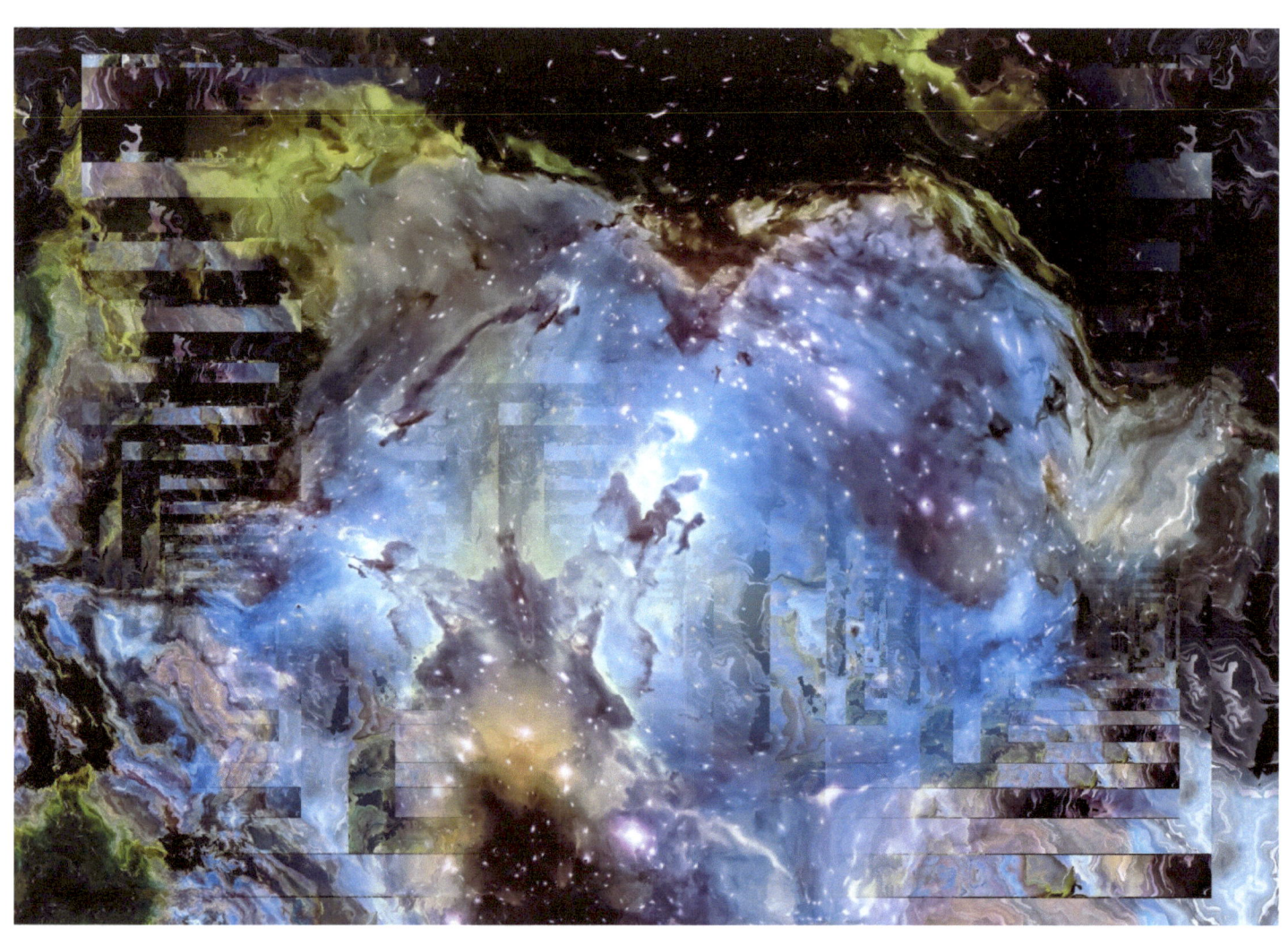

ABSTRACT WITH EAGLE NEBULA

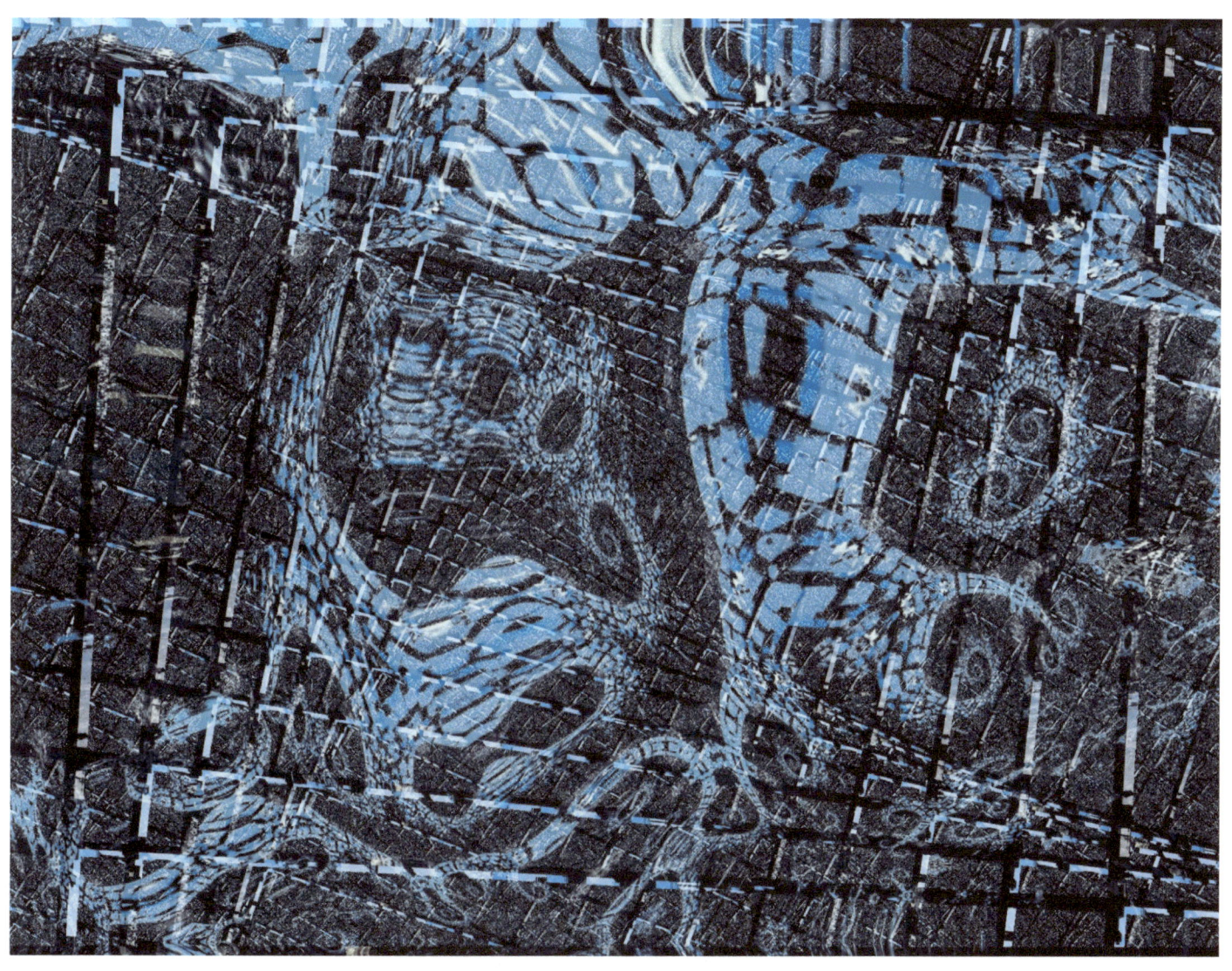

ABSTRACT STRUCTURE AND POTENTIAL I

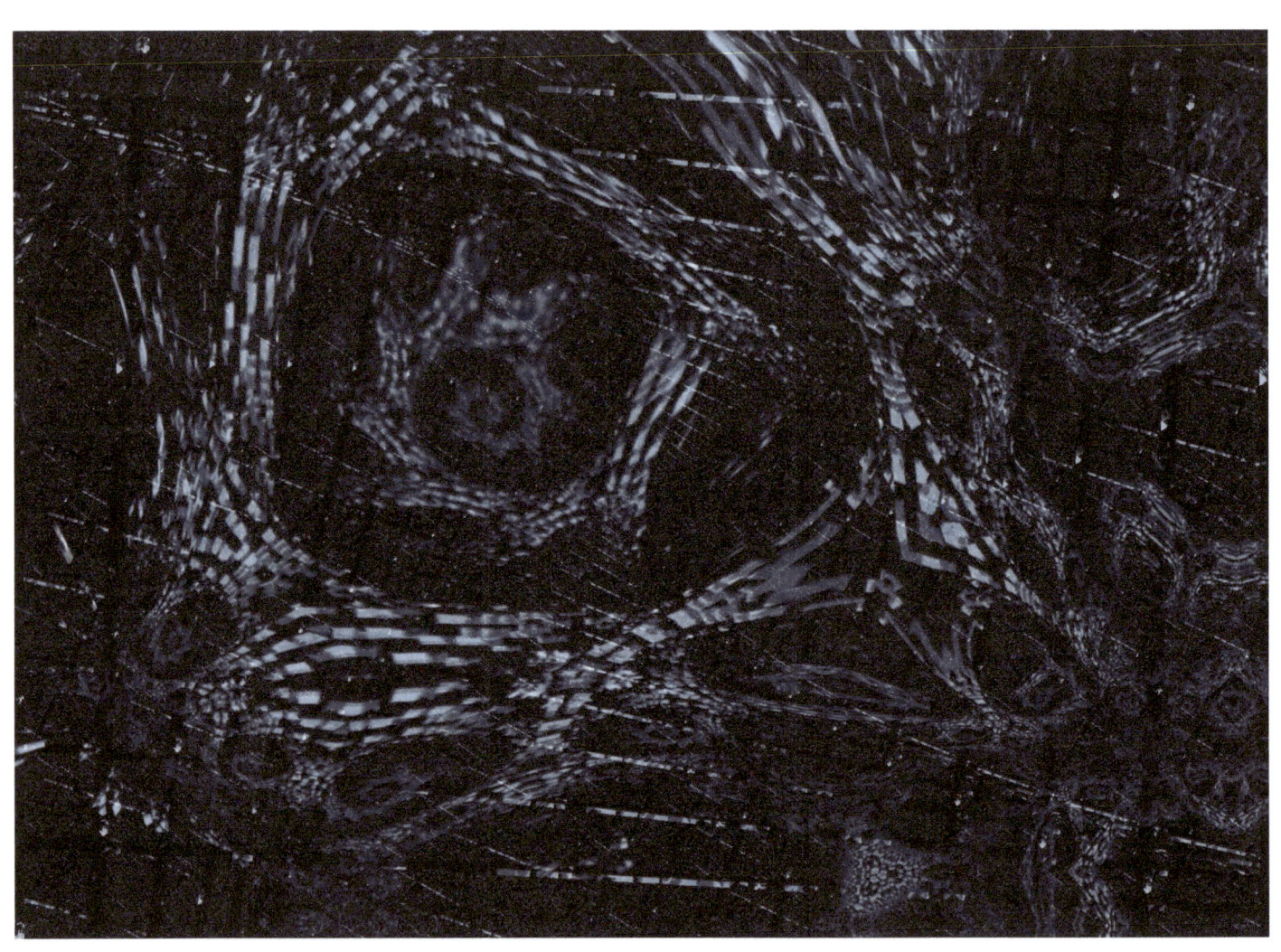

ABSTRACT STRUCTURE AND POTENTIAL II

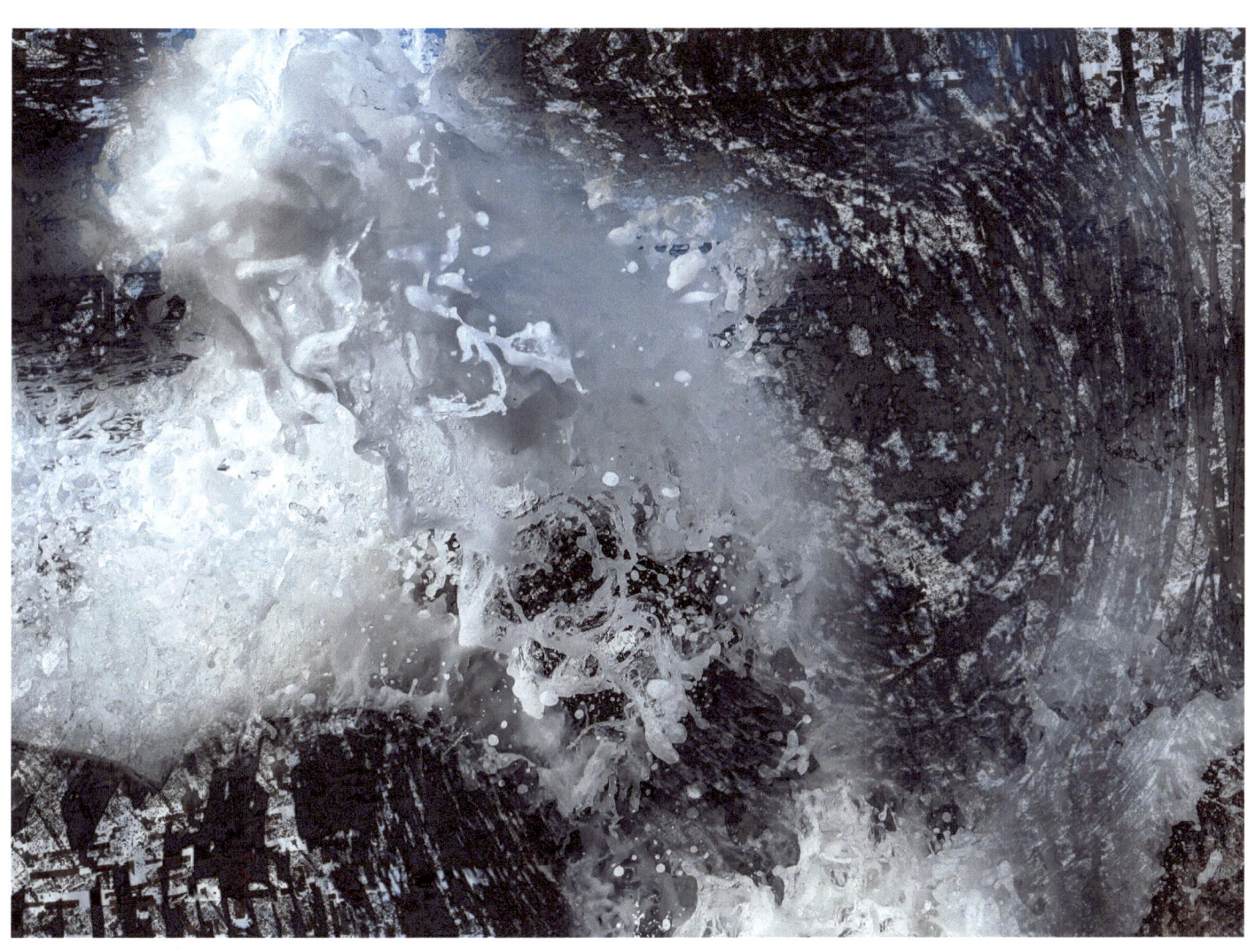

ABSTRACT STRUCTURE WITH BREAKING WAVE

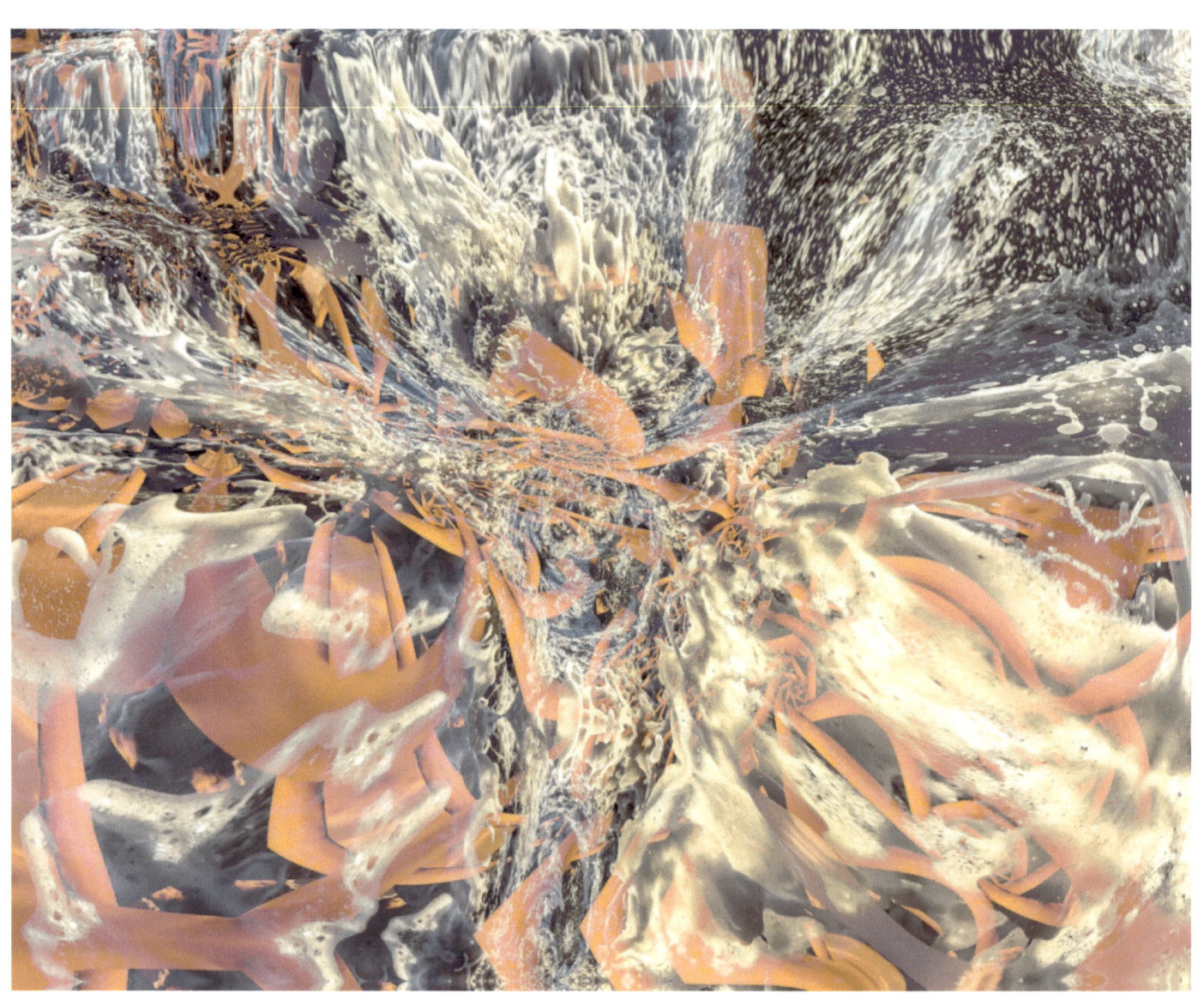

ABSTRACT STRUCTURE AND POTENTIAL III

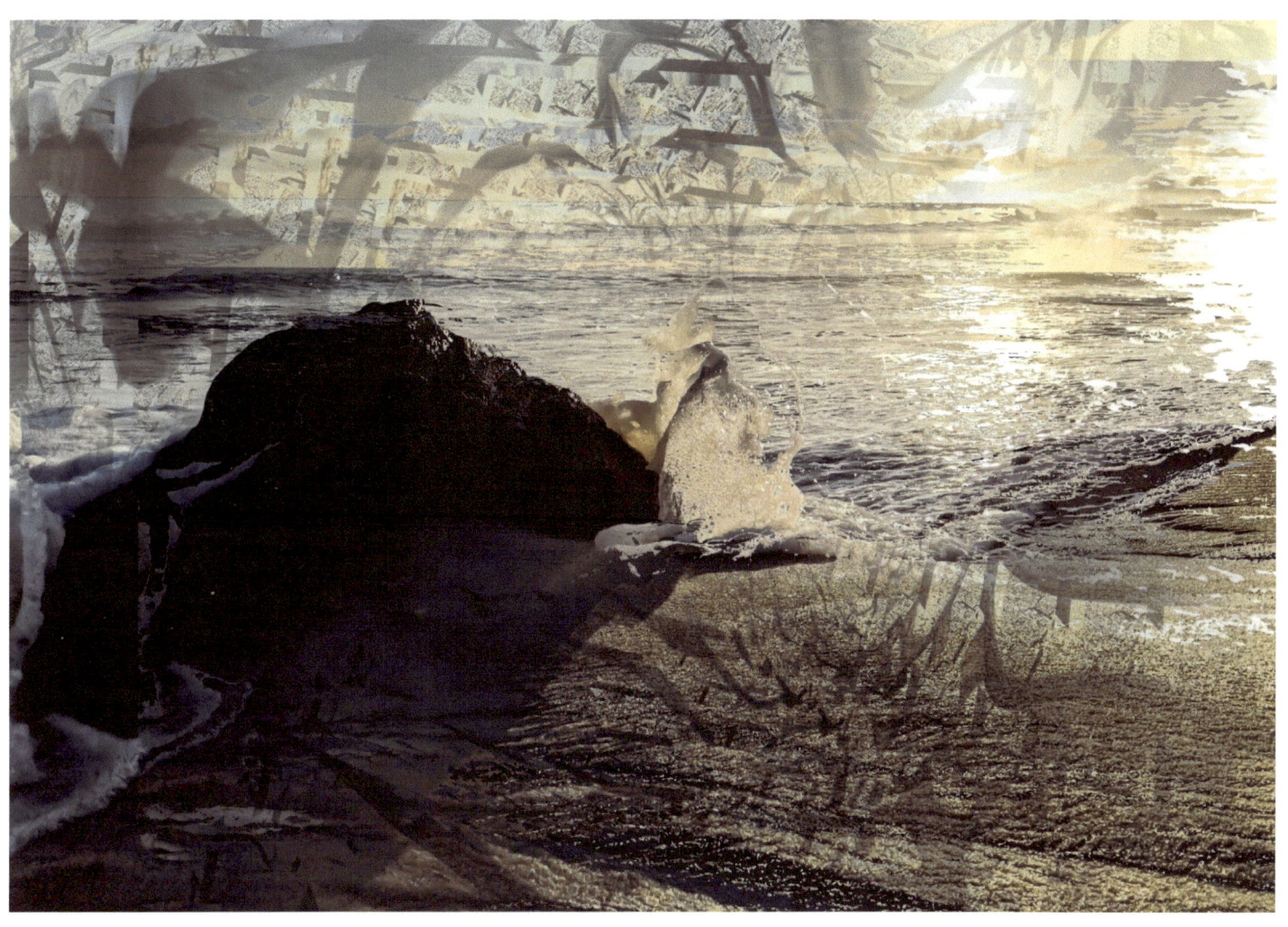

ABSTRACT WITH OCEAN SUNSET

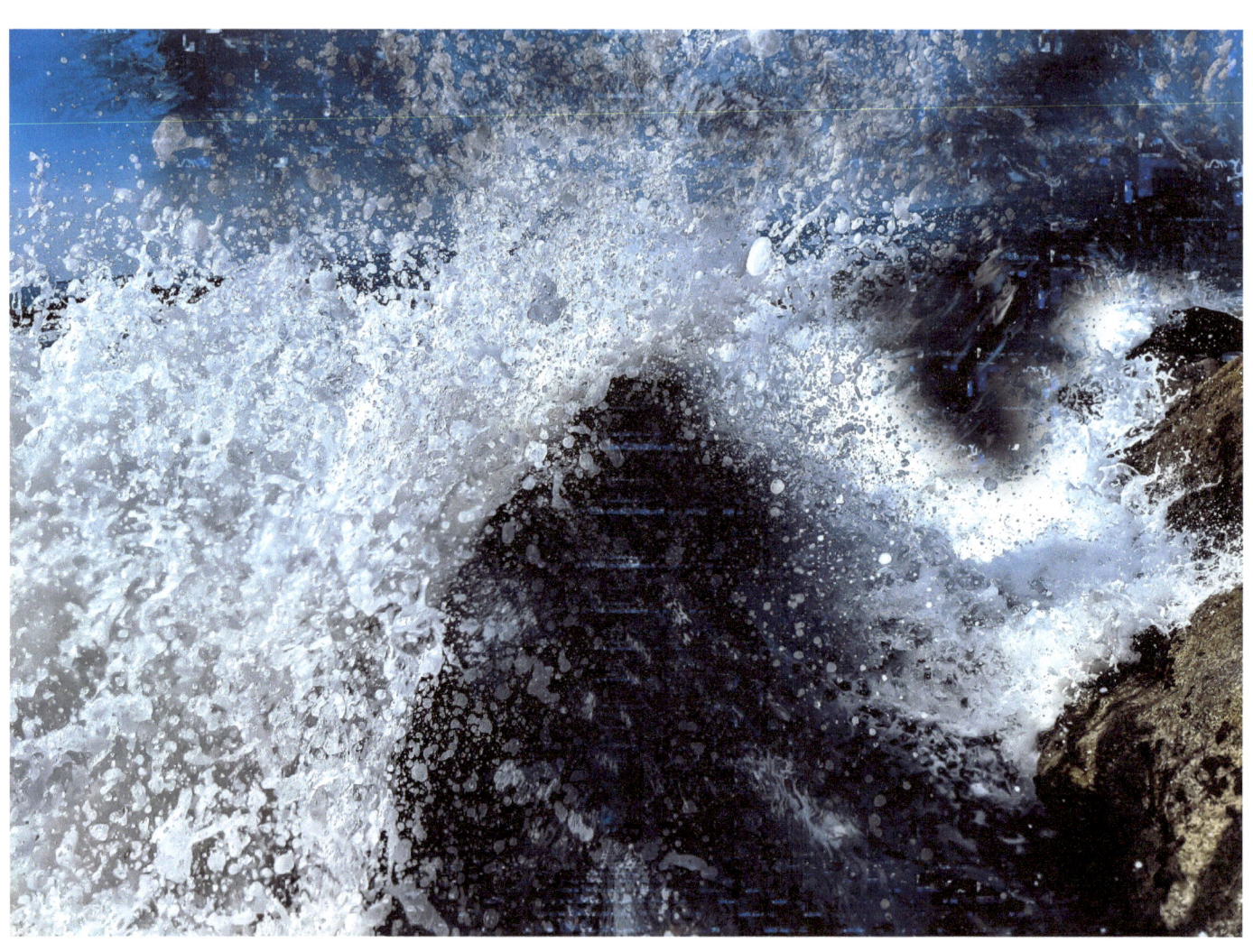

ABSTRACT WITH CRASHING WAVE, PCH CA

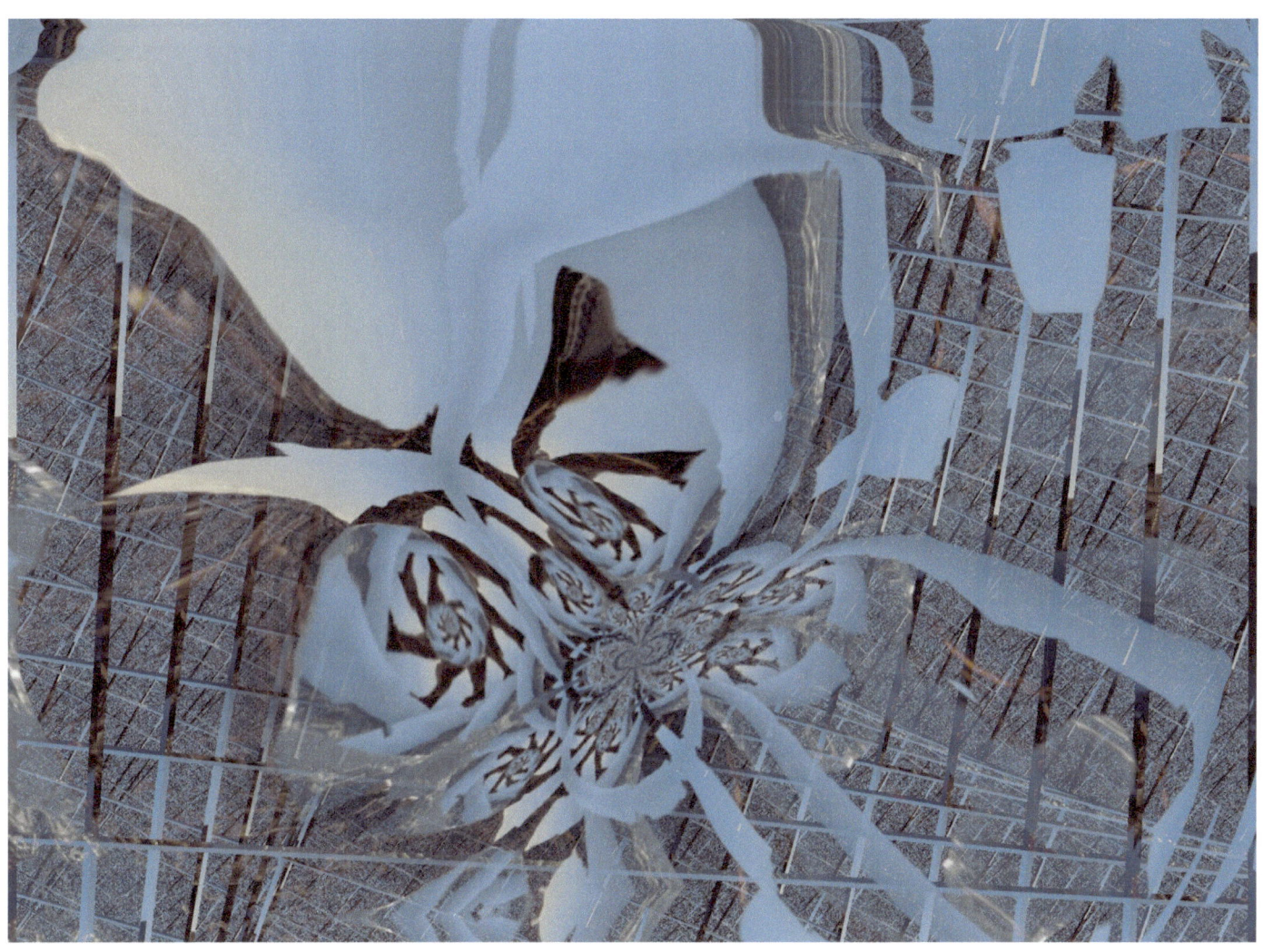

ABSTRACT STRUCTURE AND POTENTIAL IV

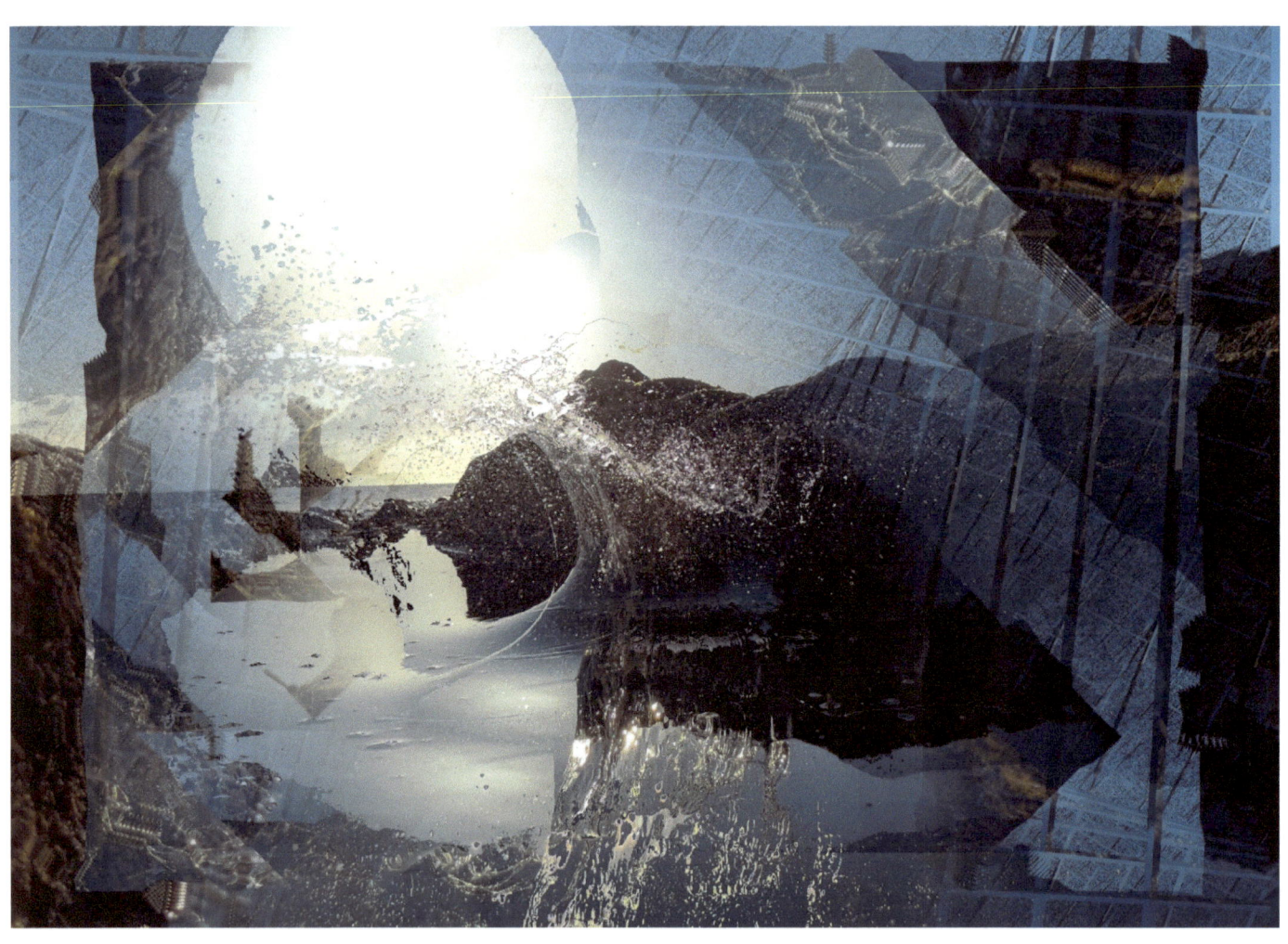

OCEAN SUNSET, PCH CA

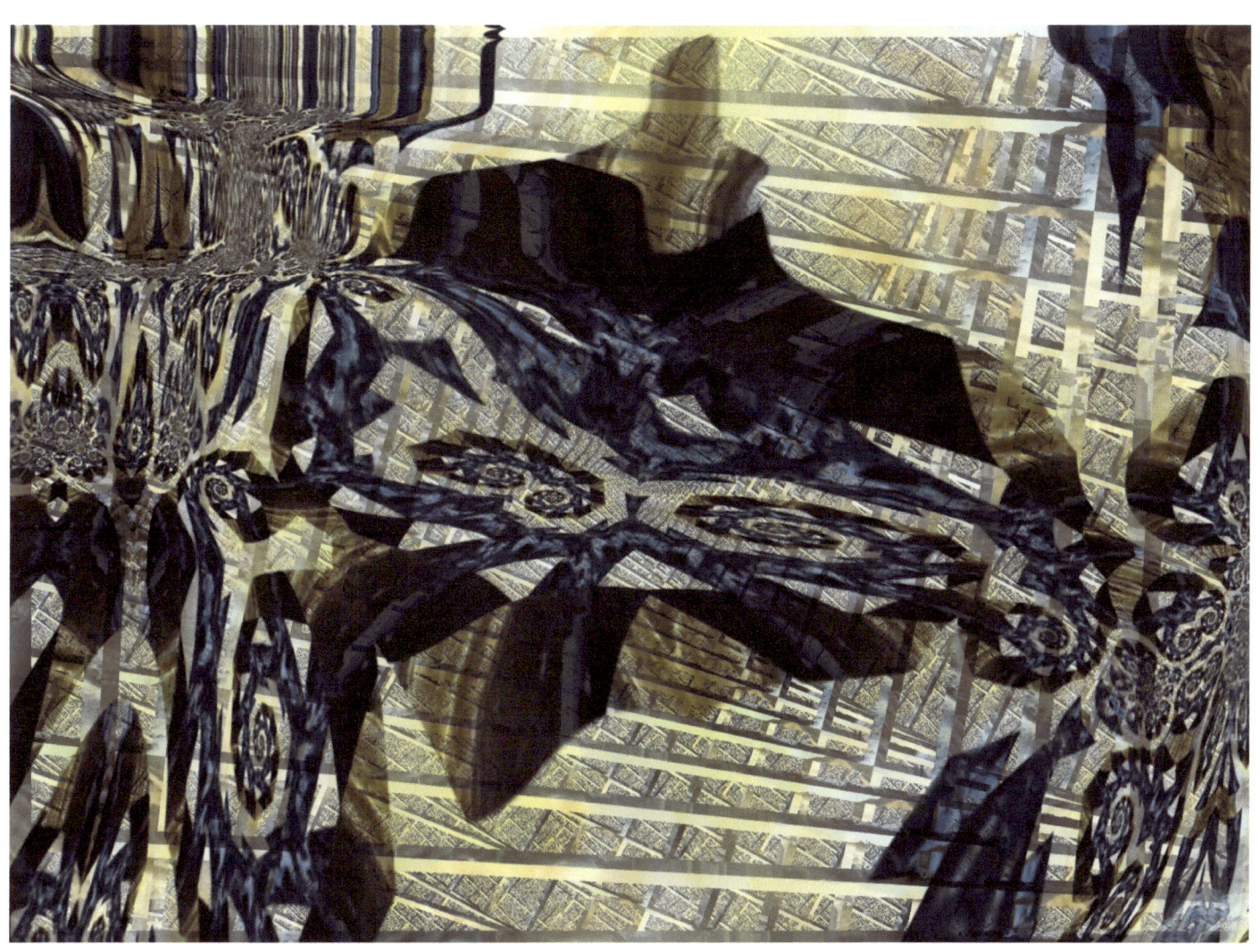

ABSTRACT STRUCTURE AND POTENTIAL V

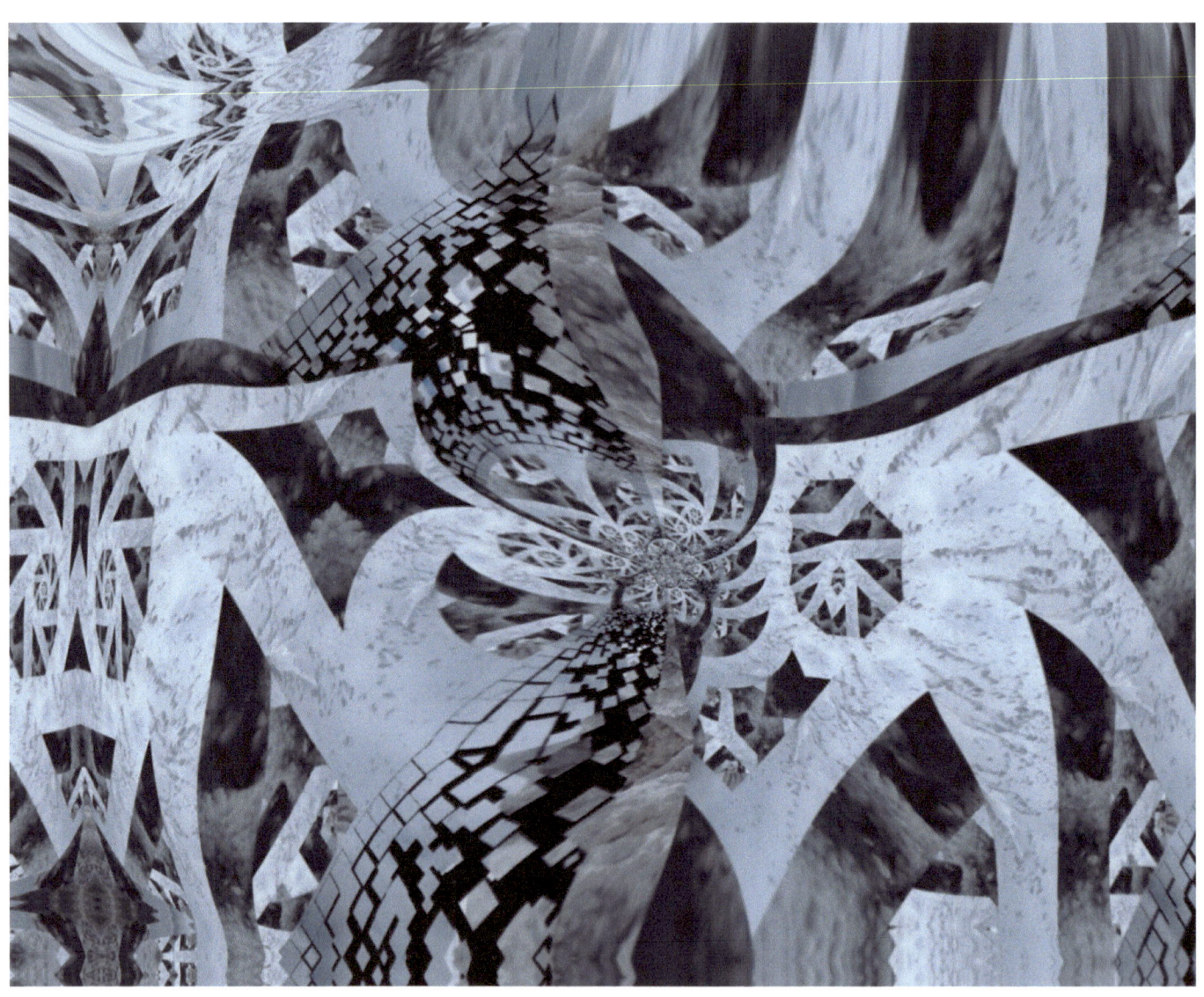

BIRTH OF A NEW ORDER

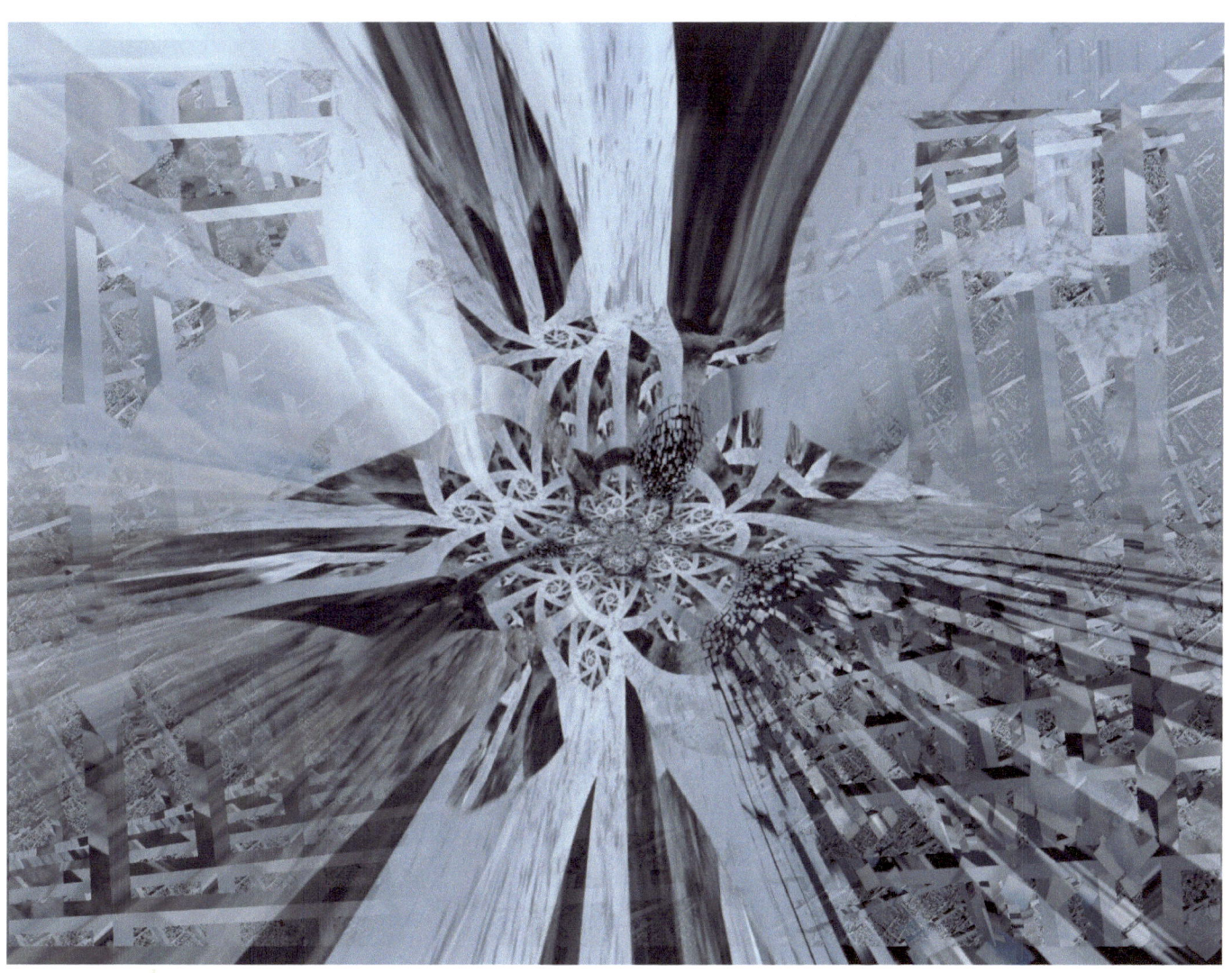

ABSTRACT STRUCTURE AND POTENTIAL VI

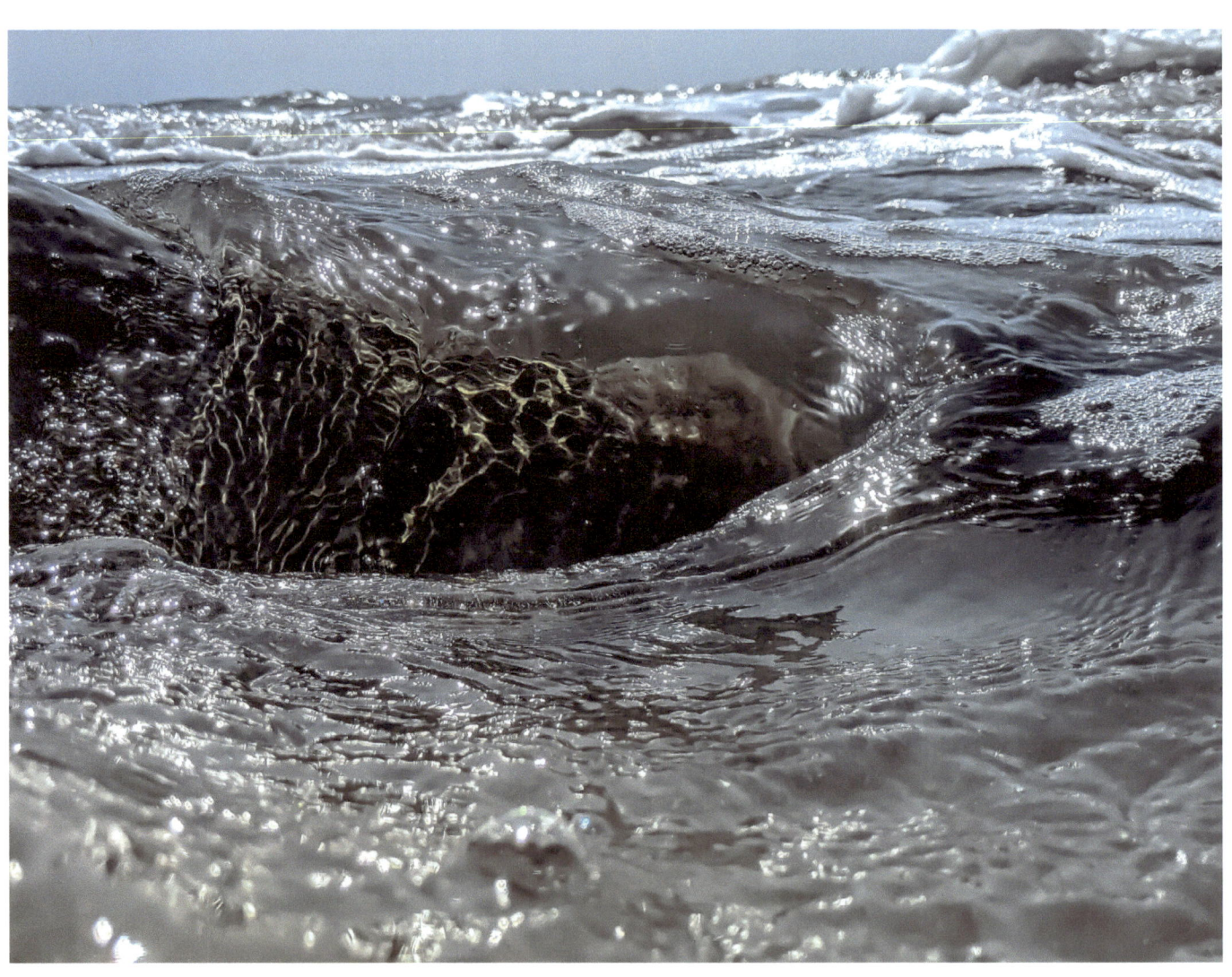

ROCK AND WAVE, PCH, CA

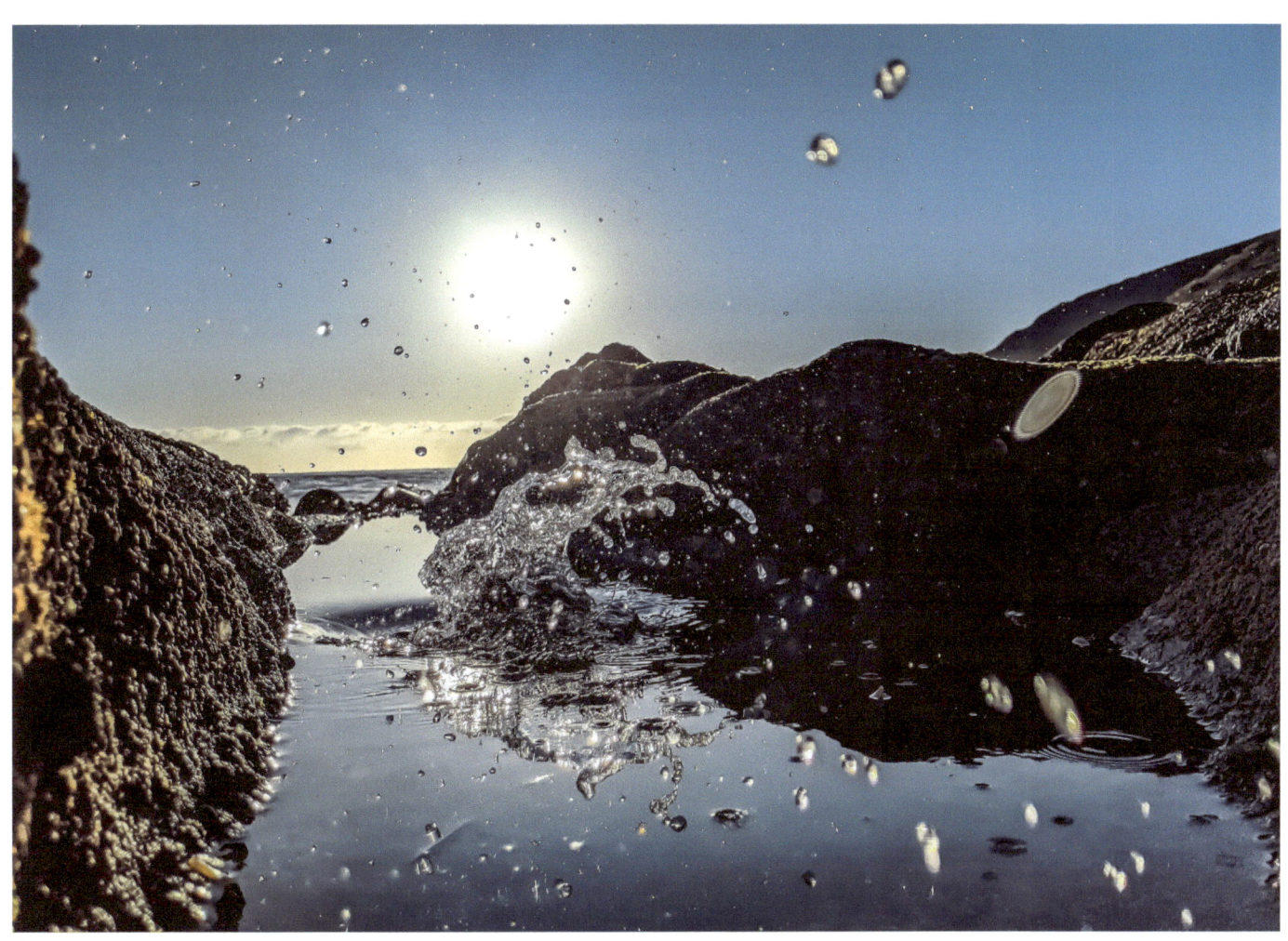

SPLASH IN A TIDE POOL, PCH, CA

A splash in the ocean
Waves of ripples -
Undulating currents
Against the flow -
Die 'ere moments have passed.

A crashing wave
Burst of droplets and crashing pound-
Undulating waves of sound
Distinct in the din -
Die 'ere moments have passed.

A drop of hope within
A word of love -
A brief spark against
Life's all consuming fire -
Dies not, until all moments are passed.

Structure and Potential
Two lovers forever in flight -
Running from and toward the other.

Potential she seeks to spread
o're all that she see,
A blanket of life, painted in colors
Riotous bright and filled with shapes
Both massive and sprite.

Structure he seeks to contain
Within a sheltered space,
All that his lover can bring forth
And yet she pushes for more.

In natures world this chase
Is everywhere to see.
Potential cannot be happy,
Nor so can structure be,
Till both find balance within
Creative harmony.

In the human world
We call this love -
To exist in creative harmony.
This love we seek to find
Under every rock and stone.
We seek to find - but not to make-
And thus we seek alone.

* WRITERS NOTE:

I don't want to end this book without leaving space for you, the viewer, to react. The initial challenge all artists face is getting anyones attention, but the bigger and more real challenge is communicating their vision so that others understand. What I have presented in the pages above are my attempt at explaining the world as I see it. I am using the below pages to offer you a challenge.

I believe that love has the potential to change the world. If you agree, and I certainly hope that you do, I challenge you to deconstruct the structure of your own life, the day to day experiences you have and the motives that drive them, and examine it. Draw it out if it helps. Then ask yourself: how can **I** add the love to change just one small part of this structure at a time?

Like to the falling of a star,
Or as the flights of eagles are,
Or like the fresh spring's gaudy hue,
Or silver drops of morning dew,
Or like a wind that chafes the flood,
Or bubbles which on water stood:
Even such is man, whose borrowed light
Is straight called in, and paid to night.
The wind blows out, the bubble dies;
The spring entombed in autumn lies;
The dew dries up, the star is shot;
The flight is past, and man forgot.
- Henry King

ABOUT THE AUTHOR

Michael Marschner was born in Dallas Texas in 1977. Although he grew up in the suburban sprawl of Washington D.C., he now lives in Camarillo, California. He is married (has been for 17 years, actually) and has three children.

www.ingramcontent.com/pod-product-compliance
Lightning Source LLC
Chambersburg PA
CBHW040420220526
45473CB00004B/1305